I HAD TO

BREAK ME

ISBN (Paperback): 979-8-9871140-1-8

ISBN (Hardcover): 979-8-9871140-0-1

ISBN (Ebook): 979-8-9871140-2-5

Edited by Emily Price Soli

Book design by Nuno Moreira, NM DESIGN

Content Guidance:

Parts of this collection explore the complexities of trauma, mental health issues, and heartbreak. Expect depictions of sexual harassment and suicidal thoughts. This collection may not be suitable for children.

Please read with care.

I HAD TO BREAK ME

by NISHA

I offer my deepest gratitude to all the voices within me that guided me, nurtured me, nourished me, and tormented me during this process. I was a mere vessel for the manifestations of this expression. I am forever grateful to my dear family, friends, and community.

CONTENTS

INTRODUCTION

When life wages war within you, where do you hide?

When you have been wounded, where do you seek refuge?

Who do you trust with your deepest fears and grievances against life?

When you can no longer trust your own mind, where do you go for solace?

When the heart longs to be broken in order to heal, can you trust the pain that emerges?

To answer these questions, I had to break every known piece of me. I had to destroy every shelter I'd created and tune in to every voice of fear. I had to embrace a long-overdue death. I had to shatter every piece of my ego, which captured my spirit in solitary confinement. Ultimately, I had to *embrace* every broken piece of me.

I am not a writer or a poet. Instead, with this collection, I have transformed my nauseous suffering into a form. I have converted my cry into a mosaic of words. I have turned my joy into scripts. No, I have never been a writer; I am an observer of all of this within me.

I HAD TO BREAK ME is a collection born from thousands of hours of solitude, in which I processed my deepest, darkest truths. The story unfolds in six parts:

1.   WARS: The battles we wage within and without. I contend with a broken healthcare system and the religious teachings that no longer soothe me. I confront old ways of being that no longer serve me.

2.   YOU: The glories and agonies of love. I experience great changes within me as a result of my loving and being loved.

3.   MOURNING: A journey of returning. I have lost myself in the vicissitudes of life, but I am determined to find myself again.

4.   EARTHQUAKE: A personal account of the April 2015 earthquake in Nepal. I see my home country reduced to rubble, and I strive to reassemble the pieces—the pieces of our infrastructure and our community.

5.   STILLNESS: The barest possible portrait of my soul. I move from the ego's painful trap to a fresh, sweet freedom.

6.   ME: A central truth revealed. Every war, every love, every pain, every revelation Is completely contained within my perception. I explore "the language of my own book."

This poetry collection is for seekers of wisdom, lovers of self-exploration, and those who want to attune to the subtle realities within each of us. My hope is that these poems offer you expansion past the limits of self as defined by ego.

I am ready to welcome you into my world. I pray you find solace, joy, and love here.

PART 1: WARS

War within me

No power in this world can make peace with it

No material comfort can resolve this uncivil war within me

No lover can appease this war

—

Yes, I suffer

I recognize my suffering rather than blaming everyone else

I suffer because I am attached

I suffer because I am afraid of the unknown

I suffer because I lose faith so fast

I suffer looking at the wounds of others

I suffer because I think I can change others

I suffer because I think I can change the world

I suffer because I seek love in others when I am the love I have been
waiting for

I suffer because I escape the present moment, living between a recurring
past and the unknown, unmanifested future

Which god will you take me to for the sins I have committed?

Which temples of god do I enter?

Which visible portraits of god do I trust?

Of the gods that have been forced upon me, which do I ignore?

—

Don't—don't drag me to the temple
I won't find anything there
It reminds me of that hell you threaten me with
The blood of sacrificed animals splashed on the floor for your well-being
Please don't—don't force me to sit with discipline before the priest
That priest chokes the voice of my god

I have been pushed inside the beautifully decorated homes of so-
    called gods
I have been touched inappropriately inside the houses of gods
I have been molested by an unknown stranger inside the temple
I have witnessed wounded smiles waiting to be healed by the gods
    within us

—

I can't perform the rituals you have entrenched in me
I can't follow rules that have been imposed upon me
I can't find god in the parroted mantras so constantly recited
I can't assemble all the goods and take them to your god
I can't seem to bribe god

—

God inside me:
What do you see that I seem to ignore?
Veil opens slightly
And closes again.

You are the malady in my immortality

You are the confusion in my clarity

You are the ignorance in my wisdom

You are the sins in my blessings

You are the salt sprinkled on my bleeding ulcer

You are the raging fire within that cremates me each moment

You are the death in my reincarnation, occurring simultaneously

You are the resurrection that sprinkles tepid water on my moribund self

I am that you

You are that me

I need to find me in that you

Does the heart lie
When it feels?
Why does the heart feel?

My ego defeated me today
I have become lifeless again
I question me
I exist as a blaze
I exist as a rising sea level

I have withdrawn again
The valves to my heart are occluded today
Congested with stagnant stale emotions
My failed state needs an effusion

Cut me open
Drain my lucid pain
Silence my dissenting voices
Don't protect me with those toxic walls
I'd rather be wounded
I'd rather face the pain

I want to disappear in this moment,
Fall and fall down,
Fall like the leaves that have fallen,
Temporarily perhaps,
Like the leaves now being crushed
By the passersby.

Should I have trusted my heart?
Is my heart to be trusted?

—

My dreams are manifesting, yet I am frozen
Too frozen to numb my pain
Countless dreams scaffold my pain
Even my tears have frozen
My anger doesn't dare melt my frozen tears
I have become like concrete
Even nature does not recognize me
I want to yell
Yet I subdue it with material dreams that have materialized
I don't have the courage to face the truth
I don't have the stamina to look into my own wounds

They see me and my aspirations
Everything said
And nothing heard
Nothing said
Yet all the voices heard

—

Freedom, where you can't even hear your breath

Freedom, where you can't taste the essence of your food

Freedom, where you can't sleep in peace

Freedom, where you constantly worry about tomorrow

Freedom, where your past continues to haunt you

Freedom, where you can't enjoy your own presence

—

I invited many guests to my sacred space
I heard their incessant voices in my head
I entertained them with my thoughts and feelings
I am seeking that space, without their voices in my head

I am cremated every day by the toxicity of my thoughts.

I need to add more oil to my fire to burn

My anger,

My rage,

My hostility,

My longing,

My endless desires.

My body disintegrates with each log of thoughts,

But my thoughts never seem to become ashes.

When will they become ashes so I can offer them to the water?

So I don't cling to my existence?

Even the water that I am waiting to be saved by is contaminated with

the toxic waste of our greed.

What would happen if I buried myself beneath the ground?

Would my thoughts find me under the soil?

—

I don't know why I complain when every luxury is presented
to me on a plate

I get fooled
Over and over again
Fooled by the illusion of my thoughts
Stories I create within myself

I design my own entertainment
Reality refuses to attest to my story
Affliction so close
I get fooled by it again
And the cycle repeats and persists

I bang my head against the sky that has no wall

32

Where do healers go when they are wounded by their own pain?
By carrying the pain and suffering of others?
Who will put that salve on their wounds?
Who can they trust to heal?

I am haunted by this 15-minute visit.
Healing others has become a venom for me.

—

This untold story
Being labeled with a diagnosis

This untold and undiagnosed story
Being checked off and masked with a pill

This 15-minute office visit

In those 15 minutes, we begin to explore your life
In those 15 minutes, I feel your pain
In those 15 minutes, you cry in that room

I worry I am missing a major medical diagnosis
I worry I may not have addressed all your labs
I worry I will forget to ask important questions

In those 15 minutes, I hope you don't ask me for a Vicodin refill
In those 15 minutes, I hold my urine so I can hear the details of your story
In those 15 minutes, I worry if I have written enough notes for your next visit
In those 15 minutes, I worry if I can give you the same attention that I
    gave to my first patient of the day
In those 15 minutes, I worry you may not have understood what I said

I practice listening to you without interruption
I type as fast as I can, ignoring the aches in my hands
I forget myself in those 15 minutes with you

In those 15 minutes, I see refugees from all over the world
Including our own refugees, who are involved with drugs, gangs,
    violence
And there is no rescue committee looking to resettle them

—

Burnout and a hand injury

This computer takes me away from healing other beings
I have become useless without my ability to click and type
Unable to touch a broken soul without this click

I have become useless to the world of clickers today
There is no place for me in healthcare without being able to click
I have become untouchable in this world of clicking
I feel burning pain in my hand after every click
I patiently wait for others to do the clicking for me

I pray this clicking does not come between you and me
I pray registration and insurance do not come between you and me
I pray pharmaceuticals and diagnostics do not come between you and me
I pray legal bureaucracy and "cover your own ass" do not come between
    you and me

I wonder how many hands are still hurting with this click
How many souls are not being healed with this click
I pray to god to take clicking away from healing

Healing so profound that it can break the pain of generations
Healing beyond time and space
Healing beyond race and language
Healing beyond the history of present illness to untold and unmanifested
    healing
This click has led me to find my own healing

Physical pain so deep
It hurts to move
I cry to a river
I witness this suffering
This pain confining me
No wine or thistle to mask this pain
No shopping for a brief rampage
I only witness this feeling
As an observer
Paralyzed by my own disability

—

I was dying every moment
I was dying being told what to do
Most of all, my spirit was dying
I was dying, and I was living in tomorrow
I was pretending to be happy
I was finding peace in healing others
Fancy food could not restore my life
Luxury was wasteful
I was dragging myself to go to work
I was forcing my very existence
Effort was needed for every task
I was dying every second to live for tomorrow
My past had already beaten me alive

Nature is flirting with me
I'm still obsessed with that text I have not received

Flowers just bloomed from dark winter
I'm still upset about the past

The tree has already forgotten about the fallen leaves
I'm still ruminating on my pain

—

I played by every damn rule you asked me to.
Where were you when I was lying stricken,
Unable to move?

I was suffocating under those rules.
But when I fell down broken,
None of your rules mattered.

I am frozen at a sterile temperature.

My every essence is lost while being frozen perfectly

Into plumed variations, and yet retaining no inch of taste.

Everything is at a standstill and cast in boxes within me to make different
shapes of ice.

This stops the bleeding within me transiently.

How long do I stay frozen in rooms of refrigeration within me?

The emotions I freeze,

Deepest desires I keep frozen.

What happens when there is no more electricity to sustain the freezing
within me?

What happens to the flow within me?

What happens if I dance to the fluidity within me?

To the broken pieces of dreams,

To the scarred heart,

To the scared vehemence,

To the untamed and unfrozen self in fluidity.

It may overflow onto the floor.

It may stink with fungi and mold on the surface within me.

I may have to throw myself into the garbage.

I may have to drain the clogged system.

Then, perhaps, I will start tasting the nectar within me that is unfrozen,

Its true essence.

—

Trees dance for me
I am still caught up in my redundant thoughts

Flowers smile for me
I am still in despair

Sky paints for me
I still ruminate

Flower blooms, knowing it will soon fall to the ground
I am still afraid to bloom

It's the same pain
Some days, I cry
Some days, I am angry
Some days, I witness it as it is
Some days, I blame others
Some days, I fight with it
Some days, I pray for it to heal
Some days, I want to disappear
Most days, I accept it for the lessons it is here to teach me

—

Allow me to scream
Allow me to face the depths of my pain
My self-created illusive pain

This battlefield is coarse
I'm not as strong as you think I am
I just need a corner to cry in

There is no war to win here
There is nobody to blame
Let me reside in my absolute suffering
Sweep away the dust created by my longing for love

Don't soothe me with the temporary charms of this world
I can't find glamour in that anymore
Don't calm me with your own vulnerability
I see the pain in your eyes that you're trying to hide
I don't recognize this world
I can't belong here yet
I am struggling to breathe from my own choking fist
I am facing my every existence

—

I entertain living in a monastery
To hide from all these feelings
To be away from people
Or more so from myself

Turmoil and terrains to pass through
Hurdles and realizations to process
Temptations and fires to extinguish
Feeling the intensity of this cry

I cry
Tears flowing through that do not stop

Together yet alone
Alone yet together
Distant yet so close
So close yet so distant
In pain yet free
In comfort yet in so much pain

—

Rain falls and cleanses the sparkling oil from the black concrete next to
    my balcony   48
I have been crying and cleansing me of the internal dirt that I have
    accumulated, hidden, and ignored over the years
I convert my vigorous cry into an audacious half-smile

—

I became like the sands of a dried-up river
Angry because my river was taken from me

Ego held my spirit in solitary confinement
It was diligently trying to protect me
I was dying along with the armor of its protection
No mountain would dare to echo my cries

I have bolstered enough courage to live in the land of unknowns without
    any protection
I will continue to live in my wounded self

PART 2: YOU

Falling for that you

And falling within me

My ego is failing on every vibration of that you

—

You give my soul a gateway to embrace me
And I find you buried deep within it

Come here
Find me
Embrace every space within me
Touch every subtle vibration in me
Encounter the hidden depths sequestered by my emptiness

I am finding me within my definition of you

You calm the pupils of my eyes
From chaos to stillness
You touch me with a glimmer of hope
In the prism's moonlight
Highlighting and augmenting my being

Dance a duet with me
Hear my inner voice
Listen to my unspoken words
Tune into my restlessness
Tune into my perpetual bliss

I close my eyes to feel the whispers of your heart
I float and fly simultaneously within the expansion of my heart
The endless chatter and voices evaporate
Leaving a residue of peace

Whisper again in my solitude
Don't allow my heart to close

—

Float with me in this vacuum
Without our minds or egos
With no destination

Twirl the moment
Mesmerized by its beauty
Fear evaporating to dew
Permeating into each other

I want to be loved
To be held
To forget the diurnal rhythm of the sun
I want to be loved in your absolute presence

—

I need nothing but your presence
I need nothing but my presence
Waking up with me
And awakening parts of me
That have been ignored, desensitized, hurt, challenged
Beyond my comprehension

Kiss me to awaken this illusive mind

Kiss me before the birds wake up

Kiss me free from the binding forces that grip me

Kiss me to unchain me from the invisible strings

Kiss me to gently enter into silence

Find me within my eyes

So we can feel and heal our suffering

Away from desire, longing, lust, and sex

Kiss me and break my bondage of being human

We will explore our lives together
We will break from this set of scripted norms

From suffering to serenity
From service to dispassion, for once

Watching our egos
We will unite into one just this once

My default is to love you immensely
And ask nothing in return,
But I request that you become certain things:
Become a poet when I am angry.
Become a healer and a lover when I am PMSing, or on my period.
Become my soul when my ego overpowers me.

When pain from the past is haunting me, love me tenderly.
When I ignore you, open my heart.
Nurture me with your ease when I am wounded.
When I am stubborn, paint me a smile,
Even if your brushes are broken.
Restore me to my default zone of love.

Nothing in return.
I expect nothing in return
Because I have found you in me and me in you.

—

It's the same crescent moon
You see it before me
I see the same moon after

Same moon, covered with light
Or uncovered by darkness
Miles away
Moon as a witness

Darkness and light coexist
In the same sky
Just the sun's rising and setting
Changes the visibility

I have seen you before
I have shared these stories with you before

Surrendering to palpable treasures,

I become godlike,

Expanding myself to the cosmos.

Through chiseling the screaming desire for your presence,

I catch a glimpse of serenity.

Again, I become human in its entirety,

Yearning for you nascently,

Wanting you to embrace me and nurture me.

—

In silence I find you

Convergence of each other into our resonance

I am swinging into you despite the resistance of my mind

Love me in every rhythm of your surrender

Submerge my heart in your tenderness

Smile at me and love me again and again

Find me in every breath that intertwines within us

Bring this moment into a gentle cadence as I dance underneath your
    vibration

Evaporate my tears and my pain with your every allure

Don't spare any pieces of me and love me again

Love me into this abrupt silence

Your glimpse of reflection so pristine
It's untouched by your flesh
I can penetrate it through deeper
Recognizing your every expression
Feeling your every wound
You also see that in me

But you are bound by rules that others have defined for you
You are afraid of these intense feelings
Yet you recognize them in our silence

You give voice to the unspoken texts within me
You translate them into beautiful words

I am the water and you flow within me
I am the expansion and you contain it
I am the passion and you unravel it
I am the muse and you paint my story

I abide your sighs in our dawning and dusking time

69

Speak to me about service
I will tune into your compassion

Speak to me about your generosity
I will spread it to the world

Oh, whisper to me about your childhood
I will be amused by it

Oh, tell me your endless stories
I will find humor and laughter in your every expression

—

I am like a leaflet
As delicate as you can handle
Grounded in my branches

I withstand the rain and wind
And the changes around me
Anchored to my branches

I wither, fall, disappear temporarily
Come back again with full vigor
You pluck me
I grow again

I become a pilgrimage for you
Shelter you from heat and rain
I nourish you
I fall and revive again with vibrancy

I may ignore you
You may ignore me

You know I can read you so well
Read every pain you try to hide
Read every subtle longing you try to mask
Read your every escape
I want to feel you in silence
And listen to the language of my heart, which I have ignored for so long
Silence brings me closer to you

—

Take your hands and rest them upon me
Draw me your feelings
Touch my lips and take me to an etheric space
Wipe my tears with your kindness
I want to rest with you in this moment
It's been a long and arduous journey

You disrupt me,
Yet you snug me in solitude.
Is this comfort worth so much pain?
My intellect laughs at all of this
And my soul consoles me.

There's something in between all this arising,
The waxing and waning of this amplitude,
These feelings for you.

Simplicity in the ordeal,
Powerful yet terrifying,
Garnishing every step,
Smothering the vessel,
Husk of hope or hoaxed impurities.

—

I was seeking your love and warmth when I was in pain
But you tore apart my existing lacerations

I don't want to say goodbye to you because I have done that too many
    times
I have deleted your texts, emails, and voicemails too many times
I have said goodbye to you, and many of you, too many times

I wish I could permanently delete your voice in my head
I am not going to call you when I miss you in my delirium
I will surrender my passion for you to my own awakening
I am responsible for my suffering
You are not to blame

May I get freedom from your thoughts and longing for you
May I get freedom from my circuits of reprehension for you
May you heal and connect with your inner freedom
May I always pray for your bliss
May I be strong enough to withstand the power of attraction to your
    spirit

Leave me alone, away from your memories
Let me rest in peace without your repetitive voice within me
I want to stay in equanimity without reacting to my anger or sadness
I have had enough
Don't you think

I want to say hello to the sky again
To the ignored flowers and trees
Can you grant my simple wish

—

Who are you without my feelings for you
Who are you without my longing for you

I used to spend my quiet time replaying old memories of us
This was my only solace from the pain and suffering

Now, I no longer engage those thoughts
I don't play those stories on repeat
I don't try to remember forgotten details
I observe the longing as it is, without igniting it

When I tune into silence
All the desires, past longings, lust, and deeper connections
Become the shadow of my past
Without choking me or pulling me

—

I trusted my heart
I trusted my feelings

Thank you for liberating me from this fantasy of you
You can never be the person I fell for
I fell for the idea of you in my head

I created this you
I can also erase the you that exists within me
The you I met couldn't be the you that's in me

I was wrong
I made a mistake
A mistake worth making to find my own nectar

—

When you have not embraced your own heart
Of course others will break it easily

I needed to experience rejection so many times
To embrace the stillness I had rejected

Give me peace
Before the illusions of love

Give me stillness
Before the illusions of love

Give me freedom
Before the illusions of love

—

Before I miss you
Let me miss my own presence
Before you arise in my thoughts
Let me honor this moment

I wish for your love, which isn't even available to you
While ignoring the infinite love within me

—

Yes, that thought I am profusely entertaining
Is an absolute lie
Let's see how long I can sustain it

—

For you, it's probably about cigarettes
For you, it's probably about alcohol
For you, it's probably about cocaine
For you, it's probably about heroin
For you, it's probably about opioids
For you, it's probably about marijuana
For you, it's probably about meth
For you, it's probably about food
For you, it's probably about sex
For you, it's probably about power
For you, it's probably about money
For you, it's probably about something else
For me, it's addiction to the thoughts of a lover

—

Every lover will reject me till I find my own light
Every lover will break my heart till I embrace myself
No damn message on this phone will change my life
I have witnessed all the messages

Crafting love for the other is an absolute lie
The most maddening lie
And I believed in that story so easily

No, I don't craft anymore
I love myself so much that no thought of a lover would make me love
　　myself less

No, I would not give this love away to anybody else
I am learning to love every inch of myself

No, I am not being selfish
This is the most selfless thing I have done

—

I am not your late-night valium
Nor your healer
Nor your shelter
Nor your best friend
Nor your two-week excursion

I am not the mother of your unconceived child
I am not a guard in your building
I am not your pride
I am not the wife of your dreams

You don't define me
You don't dictate me
More so, I don't buy your narrative of me anymore

That story is over
I don't long for you anymore
That feeling doesn't exist
You mean nothing without my feelings for you
Our contractual karma is over

—

Wanting to be with you is part of my story
Wanting to be with me is my full story

PART 3: MOURNING

—

What a misery it is to miss someone
When you don't even miss your own presence

—

You say everything in silence with the language of your eyes
Yet your words deny it

I'll miss the piece of me within you
I'll miss the piece of you within me

I want to tear and rip apart every piece of you within me
And feed them to the gods of birds
And piece them together in a mosaic for the gods to dance around you
As a diluted expression of self-loathing and pain

I am assembling me within those pieces of you

—

Does the wall hurt more
Or the pain?
Does denial hurt more
Or acceptance?

—

I don't cry for a lover

I cry for my own liberation from the recurring thoughts of you

—

I was looking for me everywhere
I was searching for me
I was crying for me

When you came
You and I consolidated into one
So hard to detach from you

Now I have to find me again
Despite this attachment to you
That I am trying so hard to fight

I have to find me in the midst of this breaking
This crushing of my own walls

How do we find each other
In our own solitude
In our own agony
In our own barriers against each other

You have invaded my sacred spaces
Please spare these spaces
I have been hiding from you in these spaces
You have invaded my heart and my essence
I can't stand your invasion

Since you have left
Your remnants have been left behind as well
I allowed you into my safety zone

—

Cut me open
Allow me to bleed from my chambers
Let me feel the pain in my heart

I have nothing to accomplish
No goals to attain or aspirations to meet
Nor a deadline to succumb to
Allow me to be so I can feel

I can face hunger

I can walk in dust and polluted air all day with very little complaint

I can work hard and get anything done

I can climb mountains

I can use dirty bathrooms

I can carry used sanitary napkins in my purse

I can face physical pain

I can live with very little material safety

But I can't face the volcanic eruptions of my emotions for you

I have no control over them

These emotions have demonized me

My mind is not wandering

My kindness comes from my heart

When my heart opens up

My mind only calculates and victimizes me

It takes my dignity away

When I close my heart my ego takes over

I become a robot whose only concern is to complete tasks

I am immensely suffering

I cry for an hour during my walks

I wail unstoppably during meditation

I don't know how to handle my current existence

My current state of being

It hurts to see you in pain

You must be immensely suffering too

I can see it in your eyes

Feeling the pain

Facing the fire

Feeling my stomach engulf me

Feeling that sensation

Nowhere to hide

Inviting all my pains

One at a time

Feeling the depths of them

Holding the shadow

Unmasking the gallant inside me

I can't escape it

Facing it

Assembling it

And releasing freedom as it is

Being broken and shattered
I wake up to devour trust again
To see the shades of green
To tune into inviting conversations
With the flowers that just bloomed

I observe this longing
And the suffering it creates
To swallow me into its crater

I am restored by my breathing
Up from beneath
Residing in the space above
This existential angst

—

Your voices wait to arise again
Wait for me to get distracted from this presence

In this presence your voices dissipate and flicker away
Leaving behind the remnants of my suffering
I choose presence over the voices of past entertainment
The voices wanting to drag me away again
For a replay of past dramas, or for future-inclined thoughts

I have been fooled by the many voices of you in my head
In this moment, I am embracing presence

When you witness your own ego's death and mourn for your beloved
What other darkness are you afraid of

Longer the days of separation
Blessings of wisdom arise
And God speaks to me in every channel

I will remind him in silence, in my every breath, of my love for him
The wind will carry that message
The sun will reflect it on the moon

—

Waves, how I have ignored you
Failed to recognize your melody
Your tedious yet glamorous rise and fall

I am similar to you
I rise and fall
Fall from my own space
And see thousands of other waves rising and falling
Undermining this dance of life

I find solace in the depths of ocean within me despite the raging waves
on my surface

—

If I had a perfect lover

If I owned a perfect house

If I had a perfect job

If I held the highest political chair

If I lived in a perfect country

If I lived in a perfect world

If I had a perfect god

Everything on the surface would change

Yet I would not be able to get rid of my own mind, which causes me to
    suffer immensely

Yes, I hear voices
Voices from my mind
Repetitive endless voices
And voices from my heart
I am unable to recognize

Sometimes I am afraid to hear these voices
My intelligence questions the messages from my heart
Makes fun of them
Pities them

Then there are the voices of my spirit
Beyond my comprehension
Meditation allows me to take a peek at them
I just observe the phenomena

—

Which voices to hear
Which ones to honor
Which ones to ignore
Which voice is my true essence

I walk away from the chatter to the currents in my body
From my tied-up emotions to the subtle vibrations of my body
Which intensify with meditation like a jolt
From one part of the body to another

I can't withstand the status quo of my mind
I can't go back
I accept the current as it is

—

Let me breathe the ocean
Let me breathe the sky
Let me breathe my pain
Breathe away from the pollutants
Breathe away from the toxic fumes
Breathe out in the open
Breathe out on the corner
Let's gather our breath
To hold each other
Away from suffering and muted existence

—

Where can you take me?
Where will you take me?
What will you give me?
Which destination will you take me to?
How many gifts will you shower me with?
Take me to my inner world.
Teach me how to be in harmony with myself.

—

In a split second
I want to spend the rest of my life with you
In the next second
I want to be in a monastery's austere isolation

—

I want to go home to the stars
Where I don't have to be in pain
Here, they think I am suicidal
I don't want to live like this
Please take me to my home of stars

—

If I killed my body what would remain

No luxury has been invented or discovered that would save me from my
    own mind

My fierce battle with it is undeniable

Toxicity, anger, and peace are dictated by these thoughts

And I join my solitude to listen to my dictator

Oh, suffering
I watch you enter my spine
Like a nervine stimulant that perpetuates with every thought
These spiral oscillations of same thoughts and emotions
I feel them with every breath

Suffering, you watch me become numb with every thought
The same damn repetitive thoughts
Like plastic bottles that will never disintegrate
The same cycle continues
I become acutely aware of these thoughts
With every cycle I recognize another depth and pattern
But you can't fool me anymore

I will watch you with the aid of my breath and sensation
I will not succumb to these temptations
I will not repeat these patterns of behavior again
You can't trick me
You can't fool me
You can't lure me anymore

—

I cannot hold these flames anymore
I am extinguishing them with self-love
I am open to letting go
I am awakening to the universal truth

I am losing everything I knew of myself
My dreams and my passion
Nothing makes sense to me anymore
Everything is a big question mark
Everything around me seems like a lie
I question my existence

I was waiting for tomorrow
To find my sanity in tomorrow
When will tomorrow find me
When will I reside in tomorrow

When tomorrow comes, I still won't be present in tomorrow

The past won't free me
Future-based cravings won't heal me
I will seek peace in this moment
These moment-to-moment minutes and seconds of peace

—

I am suffering

I am seizing from intense pain

I am a volcano erupting, forging tidal waves from a vibrant current

I am a ship voyaging toward an unknown destination, with no navigator

Just me and the ocean, trusting the currents

I am tossed up and down by these currents

Trusting blue skies, dark thunderous skies, or rainy skies

I am aligning with the forces of nature

I refuse to accept the known path

I walk to be the tidal wave

Smothering the sand

Nobody else can be with me on this journey

Solitude is waiting for me

Whether I sink or float

I will have been touched by gods and goddesses

As a warrior, I stand alone

I must go through this alone

When I am with others, I am masking this journey with a false sense of
    security

—

I miss you
You remind me of god's presence
You remind me of my effervescence
Then you remind me of the toxins within me
They want to burst out in an explosion

I feel your divine presence again
My pain streams through these toxins within me
I hold my pain for a little while
I escape into the creeks within myself

Please don't look at me with those eyes
When you don't have the courage to accept your feelings

—

No, I don't need you
Not you
No, no, not you
Everything is an illusion
No, I don't need any of you
Not you
Not any of you

PART 4: EARTHQUAKE

—

11 p.m.: An hour before the April 2015 earthquake in Nepal, as I was writing and crying simultaneously

I had to be away from the world
To understand my internal pain
I kept myself away from social media
Away from toxic news
To tune into my own news
I was tired of the same stories
The same struggles for power
The same struggles of egos
My own struggle for power

I chose to be ignorant for a while
I chose to avoid current affairs
I chose to listen to the chaos within me
I chose to listen to the pain, fear, and anxiety within me
I chose to listen to the winds and the birds next to my window
I chose to hear the rhythm of traffic
I chose to stay tuned to my chatters, my deepest desires, my fears
I chose to be this way

First week of the earthquake

134

Dear Mother Nature,

You left us powerless, surrendering to your wrath
You shook and cried and called upon years of injustice
You shattered the old buildings and temples
Destroyed inflated egos
Watched us helplessly realize that money and power are not absolute

Same fear, same heart, waiting to connect and embrace life

I arrive in Kathmandu on the eighth day of the devastating earthquake

As I wrestled with my own suffering
You shook the whole nation
You paralyzed us
So we could feel the void within us
So we could question our existence

We left our comforts to recognize your wrath
I saw the destruction
Only to realize the true beauty of my own being
You rekindled our compassion and kindness in the midst of chaos and
    confusion
I was holding on to too many stories from my past
You made me recognize my subtlest fear
Made me give up all resistance to connect more deeply to my emptiness
I cried and yelled

The more intense the suffering
The deeper the lessons will lie

Mother Nature:

I respect your wrath to heal my wounds.

Third day in Kathmandu, seeing youth saving lives under the rubble

I can see me in you
The same desire to serve
I can see you in me
I can see you in us

Recognizing one's own suffering
And the suffering of others
We will walk together through your and my pain

—

Illusory safety dismantled into rubble
Breaking decades of myths of happiness
Through their own buildings, safety nets
Wailing and despair in motion
Leaving behind materials
Nothing to save us

—

Tremors question our existence
Our mediocre living
Unexamined lives outpoured
Poles trembling in dread
Years of grudges forgiven
Neighbors and families
And strangers coming together
Harmony of humanity
Mine becomes ours
Yours becomes mine
All our egos deflated on the ground
Residing under the open sky
With one sheet and a pillow

As I sleep under an open sky being continuously shaken by aftershocks

Night is blatantly arduous
I refuse to sleep
I stay upright in meditation
Watching hundreds of people sleep in tarps
This neighborhood has become a refugee camp
Buildings stare at us with sternness
The higher they climb, the fiercer they look

And another tremor

As I examine my own fear
I find meaning and clarity
The disenchantment of materials

Ground rumbles again

I focus on my breathing
Intense panic and anxiety on each face
Only to surrender and sing to the universe
Of hope for safety
I look up to the ceiling
I prepare for my exit over and over again
I calculate the seconds and feet to jump

To an unavailable open field

Another tremor shakes me

I pull my 87-year-old grandmother aside
We wait in panic
My neighbors are snoring again
I hear the intense wailing of dogs
I practice staying with my breath

Nothing important in this moment
Compassion and kindness are our rescue
We become interdependent on each other
To manage the seconds of mellow and boisterous tremor

—

Sleeping on the ground outside with hundreds of other neighbors

142

Stars, you twinkle at me in the dusking night
Distinguishing the colors of the sky
One waiting to outshine another

You were here before
But I was lost in thoughts
Worried about the past and future
I am here with you now

lives under the rubble
livelihood in the rubble
what have we lost
what are we holding on to

—

Recurrent aftershocks shake every cell within me

144

This building may shatter
This gate may collapse
This city may become rubble

I watch myself in complete surrender to this moment
No quake can make me fear the expansion within me

Embracing physical death

I was present, very present
When I slept outside facing the tall cement buildings
Succumbing to tremor after tremor
I was willing to face death, face my ego's death, at that moment
I made peace with death every day I slept outside

Knowing that I may be buried under the cement pile
I caught my every breath
I felt every sensation in my body
I was more alive than before
I was living more than before
I was rejoicing in and connecting with every channel of my body

I was not afraid to die
Not afraid, since I was guided by my spirit
I had already chosen the path of my spirit's voice
There was no fear of dying
I would be holding on to death
If I'd listened to my mind
Then I would have died every moment

Fear could have isolated my killing
I would have been holding on to tomorrow's dream
But there was no tomorrow there
I was on the path of being true to my very existence

—

The unsung heroes of this quake: my parents

My father makes me oatmeal with raisins, cardamom, and ginger
Every morning at 7 a.m. after my yoga and meditation

We don't have running water most of the time
He makes sure I have a bucket of water to rinse in every day
He drives me around in crazy Kathmandu traffic for all my meetings

My mother makes two green veggies every day, whether or not there are
    vegetables in town
She makes khichdi every evening for me to cleanse off the day
My grandmother massages my forehead every evening
They serve me warm milk with cardamom and turmeric before I head
    to bed
Even when I insist that I've already brushed my teeth

I take them for granted
I have not spent a day with them
I get furious over 6 p.m. curfew, but I know it comes from the depths of
    love
Thank you, wonderful parents

Armor of destiny unravels
Into ripples of chaos,
Resisting and then unsettling.

Pits of shadow below me, seemingly untouched,
Bestow faith or a moribund, archaic future,
Unleashing and untaming the known.

—

I want to escape this city of big buildings and big egos
The city suffocates me physically and emotionally
Bifurcation of emotions from extreme peace to drained self-seeking for
    sight of an open space
Away from people who want to dictate my life

I seek silence

I seek fresh air

I seek water to cleanse off my dirt

I seek space to reflect

I seek space to read and write

I seek time away from people

I seek time away from interruptions

My chatter heightens with constant nags

I am not your imposter being

Let me breathe again

Let me unwind

Let me be free from your agendas

Let me be free from your imposed gender inequality

I represent both masculinity and femininity

I feel wholesome

But you remind me of a lesser being

Stop judging me

I am not you

You are not me

Don't gag me, please

Unchain me from your aspirations

And we will walk together

—

If I was light as a feather
How high would I soar
Unaffected by the gravity of people's opinions and behaviors
I am a feather for one second and a stone for another
I feel connected then I am a cocoon of fear and endless desires
I practice lightening up with each breath
I expand again
Clarity dawns upon me
I lose it again and fight for survival

Your dream of my happiness suffocates me

That route is easy

But I refuse to turn back that direction

I have made up my mind

Let me walk the path that is guided by my inner voice

I don't want to listen to my fleeting mind

Please see the divinity manifesting in this journey

Joining the universal consciousness

Consciousness that is screaming for peace

It wants to erupt from the chains of unenchanted false pretense and

    glamour

—

I resigned from my pension job after the earthquake

I lost my health insurance

I lost my dental insurance

I lost my vision insurance

I lost a hefty salary

I lost my retirement fund

I lost my primary care practice

I lost my patients' love

I lost my ability to pay for fancy meals

But I gained access to my inner self

I journeyed into the land of the unknown, which does not require
insurance of any kind

Collective amnesia

Was there an earthquake here?
It looks like we have forgotten the boisterous tremors.
Is this the place I left three months ago?
It appears we have moved on from shattered homes to blaming others,
Inflicting violence on each other.
We attribute our problems to others,
Putting faith in one person or paper as if they're a messiah to save us.
Little we seek to understand each other,
Listen to each other sincerely from that space of infinite
	interconnectedness.
It looks like we have forgotten the innate truths of love and compassion.
Did we forget our tremendous power?
We united in thousands,
We overflowed with love,
We walked to villages,
We slept under the open sky,
Sleepless nights spent packing supplies and carrying roofs.
It appears Mother Nature's wrath was forgotten easily.

—

What will we tell children sleeping in makeshift homes in a cold winter?
That we have all forgotten the earthquake?
What will we say to a child in Terai?
That we waited on a piece of paper to harbor our love?

We are always waiting for somebody to come and fix us.
I wonder what the few trees left in Kathmandu would advise us.
I wonder what the dried rivers and mountains would speak to us about.

The earthquake reminded us of our impermanence here.
In the end we ran for our safety, holding hands without attachment to
    buildings, materials, or power.

How can I fall asleep
How can I rest in peace
How can I find harmony in this comfort
Comfort that would save you

I have seen you
I have been touched by you
I have seen your radiant smile in the midst of blue tarps
And white plastic bags over your roof

The plastic bags haunt me
When I sleep in my warm comfortable room
They deteriorate my spirit
They leave me incapacitated

—

Greed on the streets has frozen our compassion
Perhaps we need enough fire in unity to melt this greed
So I can reach
So we can reach you
I am selfish
I just want to sleep in peace

—

They fix the broken building
But they continue to ignore the broken spirit within us
My soul still remains without a certificate
Despite the many accolades and initials I have gained

Ignoring my deepest desires
What will I teach you
What will I impart to you in my own neglect

Toxic air in Kathmandu

Pristine, crisp air is waiting to kiss me
It wonders when my mask will be unmasked
So the air can feel my subtle presence
It wants to experience the universe within me

I withhold this air
I fight with this air
I constrict and resent this air
I hold my breath so I don't breathe in black toxic fumes from an old bus

No matter what I do, I can't buy fresh air in this town
Not even the richest can afford it
Perhaps it's a collective effort
This pure air is waiting to kiss all of us with its vitality

Every known piece of me had to be broken
Every voice that had been ignored in the past had to be tuned into
Every rhythm had to be embraced
I had to break every shackle that was known to me
I had to break me

My creation of me had to be broken into pieces
To listen to the untuned voices of my spirit
Which was waiting to be ignited
To manifest from an embryo to full life

PART 5: STILLNESS

I have been stripped

Stripped of everything

Stripped of any layer where my ego could hide out

I am walking on glass

Small cuts are bleeding into my every sphere

Nothing but my breath will save me

I will seek truth in the reflection of broken glass

—

I am practicing all the mechanics of life, yet I am lifeless
I cannot exist in this world the way it is
More so, I cannot exist in the way I exist within myself

—

I am looking for the me to destroy
The me that suffocates me
I am still looking for that me
Is that me this body
Where is this me
I am looking for that me in my voices
It's yet to be found
I can't seem to find this me to destroy

I have captured myself in my own prison cell with indefinite term limits
Give me all the ropes you have
I want to hang all my pains, one at a time
I can't belong here anymore
Take me away from this pain
Far away to where I don't exist
Take me to the highway of lanterns
Where I can see the jade moon's reflection

—

I listen to the roar of the sky

And surrender to the tumultuous rain

I allow myself to sink into the deep sea

I gasp for air as I am sinking

I refuse to float at this moment

I allow myself to be swept beneath the ocean's depths

And find the bliss I have been yearning for, pain dissipating

—

How I wish to be childlike
To scream as hard as I want to
To sleep when I feel like it
To smile with wholesome joy
To cry as much as I want to
And forget about the cry in a few seconds

Let me regress and be childlike
I don't want to be a grown-up

—

I need a little shower from my eyes today
Rather than the swifts of my knees

I don't feel my emotions when I run
Running makes everything normal
I am addicted to running to mask my pain

I ignore the pain in my knees to be human again
To be touched by air and to fly in this moment
To feel the ground and the touch of the grass
I feel alive again with this run

—

Crying spells don't bother me anymore
They have become part of my routine
A ritual while cleaning my house
I need my own internal water to settle the dust within me

Yes, you strangulate me
Lure me to a marshy island
Lure me with heaven
But I refuse to go there
I refuse to cross to that island

I am the temptation that I will seek
Pleasure so unbounded that it sings to gods and goddesses
Demons will seek this pleasure like light through fog

I can lose this again so rapidly, in seconds
Where I wear a mask as a fiery demon
Who is seeking happiness from external forces
Forgetting to clasp and buckle one's range of infinity

I disappear
I become empty
I become hollow
I become nobody
Encompassing and holding all beings

—

There is something within me that witnesses everything
The chatter of my desires
My commotion
My aches
This something has observed the phenomena within me
    since I was a child
It is without judgment or criticism
It is like the sky, that etheric space that holds all of us
The cloud or fog may subdue observation
Self-pity and judgment may hide our witnesses
But when we go deeper, penetrating the thickest parts of us
Perhaps we can rely on these witnesses
Maybe we can tune into our own rhythms
Maybe we can decode the essence of being human

Everything seems to be ok
When you are pleasing your senses,
When you have the materials to sustain that pleasure.

But what happens when these materials are taken from you?
Where will happiness reside?
What happens when you are in pain?
Where will you go?
What materials will you try to acquire?

—

I uplift as much as I sink to the bottom

I crush and I assemble

I splash color onto the battlefield

And the colors become a thick black smog

Created by my own pollutants in my own environment

My white mountains embody truth, but they're masked by glaring
emotion

When I travel farther away from my pollutants

I witness the mountain's purity

Where spring water sprinkles onto me like drops from heaven

Quenching centuries of yearning

—

I've been calling you by different names
I don't know who you are anymore
With each new face, I am left to question my very longing

—

Facing a whirlwind of emotions within me
I become a muted observer

I am a monkish lover
Retreating from the world
Into my own cell
With a few little stories in my head

I am a lover hoarding stories of unreconciled love

—

I want to ask a million questions
When I lose connection with my presence
These intense fears and anxieties arise
I want to escape and go far away

Then I feel the magical breeze
The magical ripples of the water
No questions to ask
Everything answered in this moment

I live in this bliss and fear concurrently

My feet are being kissed and softened by the misty grass of early dawn

With each swift of my knee, I long to be smothered by this grass

Breathless, I pound the ground with my heart

Toxins and pain drip off in this joyful running

I am flying in this moment on one foot at a time

I am loving this moment

—

I exist in different layers
I am touched by the voices of anger, jealousy, and criticism on my
    surface
These voices sometimes leave me helpless
Play tricks within me
Contract me
Suffocate me
Imprison me in solitary confinement
Within the boundaries of known walls
The more I try to break these walls
The weaker and more vulnerable I become

So I let it be
Make peace with these voices
Soothe these voices
Calm the storms and the raging fire of these voices
The broken child within these voices

I watch these voices latch onto me
Tighten their grip
Poison me
Intoxicate me
These voices know I can't ignore them anymore

I ignored them in the past
Ignored them with glasses of aged red wine
With the luxury of delicate meals
I ignored the voices playing the blame game I play

—

Yes, I have ignored you by indulging in the pleasures of my senses.

I have ignored you by hiding in my career.

I have ignored you through five-mile runs.

In the midst of dark nights when there is no hideaway,

When I have blamed enough, eaten enough, drank enough, sought
    enough pleasures,

Ahhh… you come,

Playing the scenes of the past I have ignored.

The voices are tangoing to repetitive tunes,

Playing them over and over again.

Then I discover your patterns.

I realize that you can't fool me anymore.

I can't ignore you anymore.

I accept the voices as they are.

I accept the piercing pain within me.

Then the magic happens:

I come in utter silence.

Where the world stops,

The repetitive me dies.

I enter into a different layer within me.

Immense love and kindness pervade this layer within me.

I become the subtle vibration of the universe.

I become the light of the cosmos.

I embody the knowledge of the wisdom of the masters.

I carry the universe within me.

My mind entertains irrational thoughts with redundancy
I am tired of their cyclical form
I am toxified by their serpentine embedment into me
I'm shackled and tied by thought's iron fist

I remind myself to breathe
I practice being in the now
But these cunning thoughts push me into a deep dark well
I climb back up but my lungs collapse from the impurity of these
    thoughts

I resume my breath and catch a glimpse of my own heaven

When I am in this moment with my breath
I share compassion and love

When I am haunted by a misery so deep
My eyes water, my heart flutters
And my spirit awakens to this presence

—

I choose to be happy today
I choose to wake up today
I wake up to engage with my breath
I choose to go outside and run in the cold rainy weather
I choose not to entertain my toxic thoughts

Some days I lose these choices in a shadow of venomous fumes
Some days I cry
Some days I wail silently for hours so others don't hear me
Some days I wonder about my existence
Some days I expect others to make me happy

But today I choose to be happy

—

I am willing to risk everything I have for true love
Willing to risk everything for the opening of my heart
I am willing to risk everything to merge with love
Don't force me to be with a mechanical partner
I can give more to myself than any mechanical partner, who will only
    deplete my soul

I love my solitude
Please don't intrude into my space with the mechanics of life

—

Neither am I enlightened

Nor am I ignorant

I am stranded somewhere under the scalpel of both

I am afraid to go any further and fearful of the unknown

I am in a swamp of sanity and insanity

And the rest of the time, I am overpowered by the voices within me

In silence, I weave through convoluted canals in this canoe
Circling negativities and destructive thoughts
Connecting to the sensations in my body
Not reacting to or being mesmerized by past events
Just centering the vibrations within me
Seeing things as they are
Without reacting or longing for an outcome

I open up and let it be
Withstand the forces above me and beneath me
The caves waiting to be explored beyond life and death

—

Dear meditation

You uplift me when I wither
You caress me when I'm sad
You melt away my endless desires
You remind me of a gentle breeze and solace
You surprise me every day
I feel your presence so close

Why would I yearn for anything else
I trust your depth and guidance
You have transformed me, taken me to the next level of being
You touch me so deeply when I am lonely
I want to retain this silence only in your presence

I want to keep this relationship a secret
Nobody else can understand our profound partnership
You strive to connect with the depths of me every time I sit

Even when we aren't getting along
And I'm intensely bothered by recurrent thoughts
You still hug me so closely

No drama
No one to wait for
No texts, calls, or emails to expect
No guessing game about your feelings
You know exactly how I feel

You listen to me without judgment or interruption

My fear of solitude is dissipating

—

You can't entertain me anymore
I was looking for entertainment in many forms

My freedom lies here, just here, outside these thoughts
I've fallen into presumed love
I'm broken by that search for the love within me

Presence is my lover
My medicine
And the answer to my unanswered questions
This untapped, insatiable presence was waiting to enjoy my utter
    devotion

I awaken from desire,
From the endless thoughts,
From the arid desert
And self-imposed cautionary vows
To find that ambrosia:
Peace in absolute nothing.

I awaken to empty self,
To the sand dunes of aeration
And melting judgment.
Any acute sense of me dissipates
Into unbounded peace.
My mind, body, and spirit unite into one.
No longer fidgeting,
The endlessness of me shatters
Into emptiness.
I discern the subtle sounds of chaos within me.

I am aware of those tricks you play, mind.
Your suffocating steam of arising lust
Evaporates into the vacuum,
The splendid echoes of my essence
Untouched by external stimuli.

—

From this depth of silence
Journeying into the unknown
Succumbing to my fear
Feeling the now with its discourse

Away from the noise of the city
Which seduces me to solutions
I choose to breed my peripheral reality
Masking and unmasking
Pain becomes a vibration that passes by
Desires and longings become a staircase descending and
　　ascending to its lure

I recognize the impermanence of this nature
I smile at the game it plays
I become more than a puppet
I am an observer of this show

Disintegrate my illusions

Glide through my self-inflicted tapestry

Create a space for ingenuity to pierce through the mystery

Harvest your emptiness from underneath temptation

Erupt through the sediment of your longing

The seepage of the wounded self

The salve for the abscess

The nectar to defy ignorance

I churn these impurities and penetrate the clouds to reach this etheric
space

Dreams of you
Only fool me,
Only sway me
From peace to fire.
I refuse to join you
Despite the warm invitation.

I sometimes ease into fire,
But when I reside in the breath,
I find solace in loneliness,
Beauty in solitary confinement.

The reel rolls over
Its display of images
Perching one after another
Back and forth
Rewinding and fast-forwarding

The story has no one theme
There is no particular audience in this theater within me
The characters are so deeply immersed in the drama that they're
     oblivious to my creation

—

I am learning to observe every broken piece known to me
I am recognizing each broken piece
I am learning not to believe my thoughts about these pieces
I refuse to let my thoughts entangle me
I refuse to take these thoughts on my journey
I will stay broken if I continue to ignite these thoughts

I watch these broken pieces
These broken pieces do not dare to bleed in me anymore
I refuse to listen to them

—

Everything I was seeking is right here,
Right here in this moment.
Where was it?
Which shadow was haunting this presence?

I have been seeking this moment all along,
But I was lost.
I was hiding
In the depths of my wound.
It was so simple
To find this moment,
Yet so hard, so tumultuous
After the evaporated tears,
The shaking and tremors,
The trembling tears.
Everything within me,
Piece by piece,
Part by part,
Bowed to the division
I had created within me.

The rivers, swift and swirling,
Poured themselves along the sands.
But the pebbles remained in solitude.
As volatile it may have been,
As cathartic it may have been,
I was swept under.
I clung to my roots underneath,

Finding a temporary island.
And then it was time for the island to also be washed away,
To merge with the ocean.

My god has easy access
It is only a breath away
I start by honoring my own god within me
Then let's exchange for a day
And listen to each other's god
Perhaps it will be the same god we all resonate with

My god wants me to break every norm of society to find myself
The god that has been decorated in a crowded hallway would
    reprimand me for this
Yet your so-called gods broke every rule to find themselves

The closest I've gotten to god is in my own inner stillness
I am only willing to face punishment from my god, not yours

Who am I without my thoughts
Who am I without the voices of my past
What do I become without my inclination for the future

This abrupt silence
This beautiful stillness
Halts judgment toward others
Accepts chaos as it is

Noisy yet silent
I see people's emotions without projecting mine
Inviting this serenading expansion

—

I fly above my predestiny and past karmas
No remorse will web in me
Needs and a false sense of security dissipate
Fully and wholly, I reverberate through veiled cascades
And gently enter a land of unmanifested destiny, waiting to unravel
It's here to serve
Like nothing else

—

I have been seeking that you

And you had been here all along

I was simply distracted, ignoring the stillness and glamour of this

    presence

And this presence is you

I am with you in this presence

This vibrant and exuberant presence

I am encapsulated by this beautiful stillness
Resonating peace all over
I am marshed into the depths of stillness
Encountering vibrations of trusted glamour

My expansion to infinity is highlighted by the basking sun's infancy
I embody this universe like a pomegranate's unfathomed fertility
I glisten with its nectar

Beholding truth, I seek nothing
Nature sings to me

—

I spin to that tune within me

I am left with a shuddering, indispensable beauty

I align with the cosmos, becoming one with it

Becoming nobody and nothing

Like an unassembled ballet ensemble

No task to be mastered

No lover to please

Bliss becomes so apparent that I can discern heaven and hell within me,
    in minutes

I am powerless to my being, surrendering to the gods and goddesses
    within me

Waterfalls flow through me

I recognize every drop within myself

I dance to the endless rhythm of myself

Hidden meaning surpasses
I fiddle through this glossary, which does not translate into ornaments
Trusting these instincts

I contain the power
Just allow it to unfold the way it wants to
Without manipulation

Words are powerless
No human emotion can be captured by their tribute
Only rays of hope and luminosity are emitted from them
Spirits cry tears of joy as they watch this phenomenon
Dancing in utter bliss

Where pain, agony, longing, and desire bow down to the lotus
All the senses are coaxed without stimulation
Swirling and dancing in tandem
Like mother earth is being laden with so many caresses and so much
    stillness

There is no armor to don
In this perpetual harmony of moon and earth
We don't see the difference
Only the maturity of their relationship
Nothing to be said
Everything can be understood in silence

You are nameless
You are formless
You whisper and
I become nameless
I become formless with you
I can't attach a name
Or a face
Or a destiny
You are here with me
There's no separation
My longing is a gentle reminder
That you are here with me
In every breath I respond to

—

I am pure

without my negative thoughts

I am pure

without my endless desires

I am pure

without my judgments and criticisms

I am pure

without unwholesome food in my temple

I am pure

when I connect to the divinity within me

I am pure

when I surrender to the present moment

I am pure

when I listen to the subtle vibrancy of this universe

PART 6: ME

It has always been about me

Everything has to be about me

This suffering is about me

Tainted murals are about me

Admonishing myself is about me

Loving others is about me

When the glass shield collapses, it's about me

This world is about me

This worldview is about me

My aspirations for the world are about me

When does me shatter

When does me get destroyed

Will a quake destroy me

How many recurring tremors do I need to destruct me

There's the story of my life that I write
And the story the universe has for me

My story is confined to my mind
Monotonous and predictable

The story the universe writes for me
Is like a sky beyond my grasp

Today, I hold myself before anybody else
I'm not tapping into the voices of anyone
I am me, expanding in the universe
I don't need to fix anybody
The world is as it is

—

I need to make plans
To travel with myself
To travel within myself
To live within myself

I don't need you
Nor any of you
I need to be here in this moment
Just me in this moment

I gave all of myself to all of you
Gave every bit of me
Gave every piece of me
I gave easily and selflessly
Without a second thought
I gave away every inch of myself

Now, it's time for me to give
What I gave to you
To myself

—

I love me
Nobody can love me
More than I love myself

I embrace me
Nobody can embrace me
Like I embrace myself

I understand me
Nobody can understand me
Like I understand myself

I own the kingdom within me
Impenetrable to that other
Even if I dared
It would be within my periphery

That other can't bring their broken palace
That they're so afraid to lose

No war to win here
No lover to appease
I resonate to seek my own stillness

—

I was born dark
Dark as a moonless winter night
Under a full moon at midnight in September
I was born a female
A dark-colored female
They named me Nisha, *night* in Sanskrit

My mother cleansed my face every two hours with her breast milk so I
    could become lighter
My two beautiful sisters were born after a few years
Our parents loved us dearly
They spent every penny that they had so we could get the best education
My mother sold her sarees to pay our school fees
She never bought any clothes
She came home hungry after work so we girls could break barriers
We used the bedsheet as a curtain during the day

My father loved us dearly and considered us his sons
He took care of all the baby chores
I was often reminded by many relatives that my father would go to hell
    for not having sons
No son to cremate my father when he died

I was born to belong to somebody else
I was born to be an outsider
I was a guest in my own house

I never cried

I didn't cry when I was hurt

I didn't cry when I was broken

I became my own mortuary to prove my worth

Starting at the age of twelve, I'd wake up at five in the morning,
    determined to outperform all the boys in class

I spent hours perfecting my class assignments

In a boarding school far away from home, I studied standing up during
    cold winter mornings and evenings so I would not fall asleep

I wasn't the brightest kid

Other kids seemed to get it right away

I needed more time to process information

I hid a flashlight underneath my blanket till midnight to memorize
    every equation

I hated going home during the holidays

I liked being in boarding school, secluded from my relatives

When I was home, boys on the street would torment me and my sisters
    every day

They called us humiliating names

Some followed us around

I couldn't tolerate the harassment

I fought back most days

Some days I stopped breathing and stared at the empty wall in
    silence, paralyzed

I hated men

I hated every inch of a man's existence

Bollywood movies showed women being raped brutally

I lived in fear of what I had seen in movies and what I witnessed on
    the streets

It seemed my life could not be far from what was in the movies

I had seen how people lived on the other side of the world

A glimpse on the television

I had to escape that place
I felt like I didn't belong in this world
I was looking for home
Home where I belonged
Home to be free as a female
Away from rituals, norms, and imposed values

I felt everybody's distinct emotions in my physical body even as a young
    child
Pain of the rich
Pain of the poor
Pain of the wounded
Pain of the sick
Pain of the lover
Pain of the abuser
Pain of my family
Pain of my neighbors
Pain of my classmates
Pain of my teachers
Pain of the nation
Pain of the collective
These emotions overpowered me every day
Often as nausea, abdominal cramping, anxiety, restlessness, and deep
    spiritual pain
I resided in my thoughts to escape the realities in my physical body
As a young child, I hid behind the textbook and assignments
As a teenager and an adult, I escaped in the thoughts of a lover

—

I am Asian, Brown, Black, or White, depending

I am White in Nepal
Due to the last name I inherited from my father
The same last name that was frowned upon by my mother's parents

Most Nepalese think I look Indian
When I was young, I squinted my eyes every morning to look like my
    beautiful Tibetan friends

I am Brown in America
I am Mexican in Texas
I am American in Nepal
I am Black mixed with something else
I am "other Asian" on American paper

I refuse to let anyone demarcate me as anything
I am nothing and everything
I am nobody and everybody
I am tired of what you call me
I am tired of racial, ethnic, and regional violence
Whether in America or Nepal

How much bloodshed will we inflict on each other in the name of color
    or the way we look
I want to be colorless, accentless, genderless
I am one of over seven billion humans like you
I am sorry if I have labeled you with anything
I am sorry if I have not recognized your struggle with similar labels

Please give me some room to be me
Some space to be us

223

—

I have always dreaded going back home
I have returned only as a tourist
When the earthquake struck, I had to go back
I lived as a local after 16 years away

A lot has changed since I left
I'm not a scared little girl anymore
I don't pretend to be tough
I'm comfortable in my own skin
Comfortable in my own insecurities
Because I have started crying
Crying has transcended my vulnerability

Girls are not as demonized anymore
Boys are too busy in a cafe or on their phones, cruising social media
I feel safer on the streets

I practice freedom wherever I go
Practice letting go of my attachments and comforts
Practice being comfortable amid discomfort
Practice being present with every breath
Practice recognizing my ego's need for self-preservation

Accepting things and people as they are
Letting go of my resentment, of my past
I cry more often now, letting go of the baggage I have been holding on to

Every month I give birth to me
I give birth to my unapologetic, unpretentious, unfiltered self
I give birth to all of me
So I can walk through the range of emotions within me

I give birth to a renewed me
A self that's between human and god
As this self, I am not afraid of the world
I don't have to please the people in this world
Nor do I have to live the lies of this world

I bleed, and cramps paralyze me
My tissues disintegrate in me
I bleed the 28 days of bullshit I have taken into my tissues
I am not ashamed of this bleeding anymore
I give birth to me every month

—

Let me soar high above these binding restrictions
Let me be free from the chains of your thoughts

I can't be your aspiration
I can't hold on to your pride or your ego
I want to connect the dots of this world

I am the essence of my own being
Drowning and soaring inside me

I refuse to carry an umbrella
Umbrellas are for those who refuse to embrace the vitality of this earth
Let rain reverberate through your soul
Let rain enchant you into sweet surrender

Rain reminds me of my own cloud, bursting with thunder and joy
The joy of pouring down without fear of others
Without needing to pulsate to others' beats

Let the rain wash away my impurities
Let the rain sprinkle into my eyes
Let my joy sing back

I jump up and down in floods and puddles, seeking veracity in rain's
    simplicity
What a phenomenon: clouds holding such a reservoir of life

—

I am realizing how intense I am
How much I exert control on myself and others
I want to control every thought, feeling, emotion, and sensation within me
I control most of my movements

I am realizing how much of a control freak I am
And how much I continue to be, despite this knowing
I become a flower and a blade with my nectar and my obsessions

—

My period has started

I am feeling the pain of love again

I am feeling your pain, which I have been avoiding

I am feeling our collective pain

I am existing without existence

Confused

Paranoid

Angry

And feeling every emotion within me

Why does this happen

Where do these feelings reside the rest of the time

I wonder how you must be feeling

You don't have your periods

Does your pain flow in cyclic nature

How do you process these feelings

How does your ego look at this

How do you sort out these feelings

I have the courage to be single

I have the courage to walk alone

I have the courage to cry alone

I have the courage to eat alone

I have the courage to be sick alone

I have the courage to travel alone

I have the courage to go to bed alone

I have the courage to wake up alone

I have the courage to live and die alone

I am not going to be sad for tomorrow

I have stopped holding on to yesterday's resentments

I am sorry you can't tell me what to do or what is possible

I am honoring my intuitive voices, which may break the norm

I roar, tuning into them

I can't hold space for my limited mind's way of living

All I know is today's truth

And I choose to embrace it now

—

Yes, you are worried about me
Because I have left my previous life
I am also worried about you
But I let it be

You will find your path
When you are ready
Please don't worry about mine

Looks like this pain is seeking nourishment from me

233

Come, pain
I will soothe you

Come, pain
I will listen to you

Come, pain
I will savor you

Come, oh, come to me
Come into my arms

I will cuddle you
I will love you again

—

I retire every day

I have given up my 401k to retire

I have given up my pension to retire

I have given up my career to retire

I have retired to embrace life

I choose to retire every hour

I retire to fall in love with the smell of veggies that I cook

I retire to taste my food

I retire to experience the sunset

I retire to hear the emptiness in my room

I find luxury in so-called monotonous routines

The same streets and plants look new to me on every walk

I find the finest luxury in my every breath

I choose to retire every day

For I may not be here to retire tomorrow

What else can I read now

235

I am deciphering the language of my own book
I am starting to recognize the stories within me

Some days the characters are in flow, and I understand them
Other days I don't have the patience to read my own book

What else should I read
When the most important book is within me

I need the language to interpret the pages within me
I bow down to the author of this book

—

Earth is my country

Its dimensions are my joy

Don't limit me with the boundaries of your mind

Don't confine me to the space of a so-called nation

I just need a small, clean place to dance

To enjoy nature's bountiful essence

To live in harmony

But first, I need to be in harmony with myself

—

Rain is here again, and it was here before
It witnessed the bursting of my clouds
The floods we created for each other

The sun is hiding at the moment, covered by clouds
There is no wanting
No waiting
No counting days

I am in love with me
I am in love with every pain in me
Every rejection within me
I am simply in love with this moment
Each drop of rain sprinkles joy in me
Each droplet brings me closer to the sun within me

TO CONTACT NISHA

Please send her an email at this address:
expressionsofnisha@gmail.com

Website: www.expressionsofnisha.com

www.ingramcontent.com/pod-product-compliance
Lightning Source LLC
Chambersburg PA
CBHW051226130726
47988CB00001B/240